FOCUS ON

REPTILES

STEVE PARKER

SHOOTING STAR PRESS

This edition produced in **1994** for
Shooting Star Press Inc
230 Fifth Avenue
Suite 1212
New York, NY 10001

Design	David West Children's Book Design
Designer	Steve Woosnam-Savage
Series Director	Bibby Whittaker
Editor	Jen Green
Picture Research	Emma Krikler
Illustrator	Dave Burroughs

© Aladdin Books Ltd 1993

Created and produced by
Aladdin Books Ltd
28 Percy Street
London W1P 9FF

*First published in the
United States in 1993 by*
Gloucester Press

ISBN 1-56924-049-3

Printed in Belgium

INTRODUCTION

Most people shy away from reptiles, from lurking crocodiles, to slow-moving turtles and tortoises, and darting lizards and snakes. Yet they are an ancient group of animals that have been on Earth for over 300 million years. Fossils trace their evolution through the great Age of Reptiles, which ended in a mysterious mass extinction about 65 million years ago. However, some reptile types survived. Today they live in nearly all habitats on Earth, from mountainsides to forests, deserts and seashores. This book explores the natural world of reptiles, to show how they feed, move, and breed. It also provides information about reptiles related to the topics of geography, literature, history, math, science, and art, as shown here.

Geography

The symbol of the planet Earth indicates geographical facts. People from different parts of the world view reptiles very differently. Some see them as friends, or foes, or tasty meals.

Language and literature

An open book is the sign for activities and information about language and literature. These sections look at the legends, proverbs, and sayings in books and stories involving reptiles, from cunning serpents to mythical dragons.

Science and technology
The microscope symbol indicates science information or activities. These sections discuss how reptiles fare in the face of human persecution. Some of the big reptiles are endangered species.

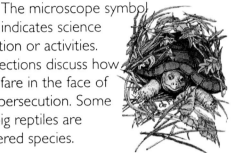

History
The sign of the scroll and hourglass indicates historical information. These sections explore how lizards, snakes, and other reptiles have been viewed through history, especially in tropical lands where reptiles are common.

Math
Activities and information related to mathematics are indicated by the symbol of the ruler, protractor, and compasses. The puzzle of the race between Achilles and the tortoise has challenged mathematicians for centuries. It is said to have been invented by the Ancient Greek philosopher, Zeno.

Art, craft, and music
The symbol showing a sheet of music and art tools signals information about arts, crafts, and music. Reptiles feature regularly in popular culture, from songs about evil crocodiles to cartoons about turtle heroes.

CONTENTS

WHAT ARE REPTILES?

There are probably more than 10 million different kinds, or species, of animals in the world. About 6,500 are reptiles – 'cold-blooded' creatures with a bony internal skeleton and scaly skin, that breed by laying eggs. Despite their small proportion of total animal species, reptiles are one of the best-known animal groups. They include slithering snakes, speedy lizards, slow tortoises, flippered turtles, and fearsome crocodiles. Those giants of the distant past, the dinosaurs, were also reptiles.

Reptile eggs

Reptiles are vertebrates – animals with backbones. Like another group of vertebrates, birds, they lay tough-shelled eggs. The shell houses and protects the baby animal as it develops inside, using the food store in the egg known as yolk. The eggs of turtles, snakes, and most kinds of lizards have tough, leathery, slightly flexible shells. Those of tortoises, crocodiles, and lizards such as geckoes have hard, brittle shells, more like a bird's egg. However, some lizards and snakes do not lay eggs. The young develop inside their mother and are born fully formed.

Hatching

Baby reptiles have a hard, horny scale on the mouth, called the egg tooth. They use it to crack their way out of the egg.

The lizard group

There are about 3,750 species of lizards, from tiny wall and sand lizards to big, sturdy monitors and iguanas. Lizards are the most widespread reptile group.

The crocodile group

There are about 22 species of crocodiles, alligators, caimans, and gavials, called crocodilians. They have powerful tails and mostly live in swamps, lakes, and rivers.

A reptile puzzle

The worm lizards are a small group of reptiles, with about 140 species. Neither worms nor lizards, they are in a reptile group of their own, called the amphisbaenids. Most have no legs and live in tropical and subtropical places, burrowing in the soil of forests to prey on worms, insects, and other creatures. The biggest amphisbaenids are 30 ins (75 cms) long.

The skeleton

The skeleton of a reptile is similar to other vertebrates, being composed of a skull, a line of bones called vertebrae making up the spinal column, and four legs. The vertebrae carry on past the hips to form the tail.

Skull

Leg bones

Main vertebrae (backbones) of spinal column

Front foot bones

Dragons galore

Myths, legends, and stories from all over the world feature dragons, sometimes called 'great worms,' The typical dragon is a reptile-like creature. It has scaly skin, breathes fire, flies on vast wings, guards stolen treasure, attacks humans, and is evil and cunning. One of the most famous is Smaug, the huge and terrible dragon from J R R Tolkien's exciting folk story *The Hobbit*, written in 1937.

Inside a reptile

A reptile such as this crocodile has all the main internal parts common to other vertebrate animals, like frogs, birds, or mammals such as yourself. These include a brain, heart, stomach, intestines, kidneys, and the bones of the skeleton.

The snake group

There are about 2,400 species of snakes, from tiny thread snakes to huge pythons. They have long, slim, flexible bodies, and most lack all traces of legs.

The turtle group

There are about 240 species of turtles, tortoises, and terrapins, called chelonians. Many have domed shells of bone and horn.

Snakeless zone

The island of Ireland has no snakes. Christian legend says that they were banished by Saint Patrick (389-461 AD), patron saint of Ireland, because they were evil. A more likely biological explanation is that snakes have never managed to spread to Ireland from mainland Britain because of the wide barrier of the Irish Sea.

REPTILES OF THE PAST

The first reptiles appeared on Earth about 340-330 million years ago. They probably came about by evolving from amphibians, a group of animals that had appeared 40 million years earlier. These first reptiles resembled small lizards. Their hard-shelled eggs allowed them to become independent of water, unlike amphibians, which had to lay their jelly-covered spawn (eggs) in water. So reptiles could spread and evolve across the dry land. They became the dominant animal group in the world, until a mysterious disaster occurred 65 million years ago.

The Age of Reptiles

Reptiles ruled the land, sky, and sea for over 150 million years. There were numerous groups, most of which have now died out. One of the main groups was the dinosaurs, which lived on land. Another reptile group, the pterosaurs, soared through the air (see fossil above left). Their front legs became wings, with a thin wing "skin" held out by very long finger bones. In the water swam ichthyosaurs, which looked similar to today's dolphins, and sharp-toothed mosasaurs.

These dinosaurs lived during the Cretaceous period. Palaeoscinus and Hypsilophodon were plant-eaters. Deinonychus were meat-eaters and hunted in packs.

Palaeoscinus

Deinonychus

The fossil-hunters

The first fossils of dinosaurs and other extinct reptiles were recognized and studied in the 1820's. Gradually scientists realized that reptiles had been very numerous and widespread in prehistoric times. In the 1920's a fossil-hunting expedition found the remains of hundreds of dinosaurs and their fossilized eggs (below) in the Gobi Desert in Asia.

Mythical reptiles

Several deep lakes around the world have legends about them, saying that prehistoric reptiles still live there. One is Loch Ness, in Scotland, where various people claim to have seen and photographed a large monster with a small head, long neck, wide body, and flipper limbs.

Reptile cousins
It is thought that birds evolved from small, dinosaur-type reptiles over 150 million years ago.

Reptile evolution
Several major reptile groups died out in a mysterious catastrophe, 65 million years ago. A huge meteor may have crashed into the Earth and thrown up a dust cloud that blotted out the Sun. No one knows why some groups of reptiles survived the catastrophe and still live on today.

Fish

Amphibians

Ichthyosaurs

Plesiosaurs and pliosaurs

Mosasaurs

Pterosaurs

Dinosaurs

Crocodiles

Birds

Snakes

Lizards

Tuatara

Turtles

Hypsilophodon

A 'living fossil'
The tuatara (below) looks like a lizard, but is not. It is the only surviving member of a reptile group, which died out by 65 million years ago. Tuataras are very rare and live on just a few rocky islands around New Zealand. Some live to an amazing age for a fairly small animal, over 100 years. These creatures give scientists many clues about prehistoric life.

SHAPE AND MOVEMENT

Some kinds of reptiles, such as tortoises, move only slowly; others, such as many lizards, use great speed to escape predators hunting them for food. The bodies of reptiles are adapted to suit the environment in which they live. Reptiles crawl, run, swim, burrow, climb, and even fly! Even snakes, which have no legs at all, can move fast on the ground, in the water, and through the branches.

Basic body plan

The lizard has a body plan common to many reptiles: a long, slim body and tail, and four legs that sprawl out sideways. It moves by making stepping movements with its legs, and also by arching its body. Most snakes also use the body-curving method of movement. They move forward by throwing the body into a continuing series of S-shaped curves, a method known as serpentine locomotion.

Gecko toe
A gecko's toe pad has ridges with tiny bristles that can grip smooth surfaces.

Flying dragons?

The flying dragon is a type of lizard from Southeast Asia. It is not a true flier, but can glide through the air. The flying dragon has a flap of loose skin along each side of its body, which can be held out by bony ribs extending from its chest. On these 'wings' the lizard can leap from a tree branch and glide 66 ft (20 metres) or more. It usually does this to escape from danger.

Walking up walls

Gecko lizards can grip very well, climb up walls and windows, and even run upside down across ceilings. Geckoes are welcome guests in many houses in tropical areas, since they eat flies and other pests.

Sidewinding

Some snakes move sideways, by throwing the body in S-shaped curves to the side. This is effective in soft sand, when serpentine locomotion would not work well against loose sand grains. The African horned viper and American sidewinder use this method, leaving a series of ridged marks like tire tracks.

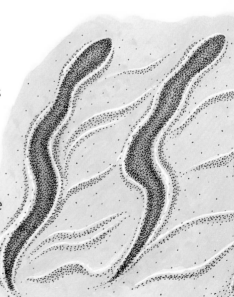

Two-legged race

Several types of lizards can rear up and run on their back legs for a short distance. One is the sand monitor, a large lizard of the Australian outback. It scurries along so fast that it is also known as the racehorse monitor. Another is the basilisk lizard (left), from tropical areas in the Americas. It has strong back legs and very long, widespread toes with fringes of scales, that spread its weight well. It can run over floating water lily leaves, and even over the water's surface for a short distance. As it slows down, it sinks into the water and dives below the surface, staying there for a minute or more. It does this to escape predators.

Catching the tortoise

Zeno's paradoxes are mathemetical puzzles that seem impossible, but may be true. Named after Zeno, an Ancient Greek philosopher, one concerns a race between the Greek hero Achilles and a tortoise. Achilles runs ten times faster than the tortoise; the tortoise has a head start of 10 units – say, yards. Achilles runs 10 yards, but the tortoise has moved on one yard, So Achilles runs that yard, but the tortoise has now gone 3.5 inches. Will Achilles ever catch the tortoise?

Lizard locomotion

As a lizard walks, it arches its body around to one side, and holds up the front foot on the other side. This moves the foot further forward, compared to just the leg movement alone. However, small lizards run so fast that these movements are hard to see clearly. The same method is more easily seen in crocodiles.

Snake-columns

Many peoples around the world have used animal shapes as the basis for their art, design, and architecture. The Mayan people flourished in what is now Mexico, especially in the period 500-900 AD. They designed stone columns based on an S-shaped snake, to hold up temples and doorways.

Mayan serpent carving

SCALES AND SKIN

One of the typical features of a reptile is its scaly skin. On most reptiles the scales are numerous, small, and overlapping. Like a suit of armor made from linked chain mail, they form a tough but flexible covering over almost the entire body. This allows the reptile to bend its body and limbs, so that it can move about. At the same time, the scales give good protection against drying out, and from the teeth and claws of enemies. In most reptiles, the scales are replaced singly or in patches as they wear. In snakes, however, the whole skin is usually shed at once, a process called sluffing.

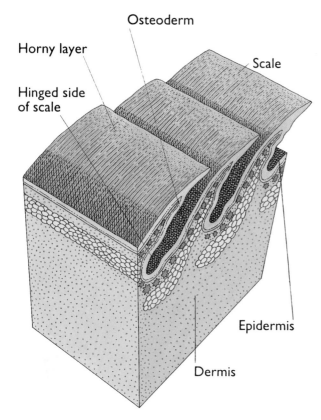

Osteoderm

Horny layer

Scale

Hinged side of scale

Epidermis

Dermis

Scale structure
Each reptile scale is made of a hard, horny material called keratin, the same substance that forms your own nails. The scale is a thickened plate of keratin set within the outer skin layer, or epidermis. It has a flexible hinge area along one side, so that it can tilt and twist slightly when the animal moves. In crocodiles and many lizards, there are additional plates of bone called osteoderms, set deeper in the skin. These strengthen and reinforce the scale layer above. Below is the dermis, containing blood vessels and nerves.

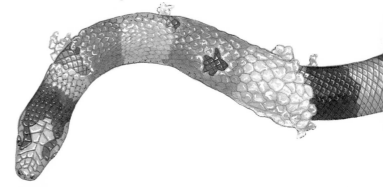

Useful skins
Since prehistoric times, people have used the tough, strong skins of reptiles for many purposes. They made the skins into hard-wearing purses, belts, boots, shoes, and coats. The colors and patterns of reptile skins are very beautiful. In some countries people believe that they gain strength by wearing the skin of a powerful animal such as an alligator. However, the reptile skin trade caused many species to become rare. Today it is controlled by laws.

New skin for old

As with your skin, reptile scales wear away. They are replaced as cells in the base of the epidermis multiply, forming new scales. When sluffing its skin, a snake rubs itself against rocks and twigs to pull off the old layer, revealing the ready-formed skin beneath.

Suits of armor

Through the ages, people have tried to make suits of armor that give the same all-over protection as reptile scales. However, the armor was rarely as light or as flexible as the natural reptilian version. In Europe, suits of armor were made from plates of metal, as shown here. In China and Japan, it included sheets of thick leather. Perhaps the most effective armor was chain mail, formed from small metal rings looped together.

The gila monster is a lizard with curious rounded, bead-shaped scales.

The armadillo lizard has big, spiky scales for protection and can roll into a ball to defend itself from predators.

The rattler's rattle

The poisonous rattlesnake shakes its tail rattle very fast to make a buzzing or rattling noise, that warns other animals to keep away. The rattle is formed from large tail scales that have remained behind when previous skins were shed. The scales are linked loosely together, the bent-over end of one fitting into a circular groove in the next. There is a story that the longer the rattle, the older the rattlesnake. However, scales sometimes break off the rattle by accident. So rattle length is only a rough guide to the snake's age.

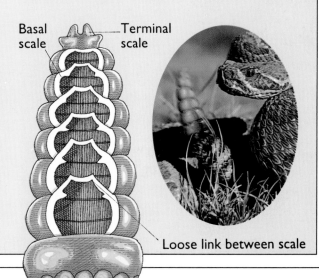

Basal scale

Terminal scale

Loose link between scale

COLOR & CAMOUFLAGE

Throughout the animal world, creatures use body colors and patterns to blend in with their surroundings and merge with the background. This is called camouflage. It helps animals to hide if they are prey, being hunted by sight. It also helps them to creep up unseen on a victim, if they are hunters. The bodies of many reptiles are dull brown or green in color, to match the soils and vegetation where they live. A few are very brightly colored, to warn other animals that they are dangerous, or to advertise for mates at breeding time.

Shape
Shape is important in camouflage. The vine snake has a slim body. It resembles a vine or creeper on a tree.

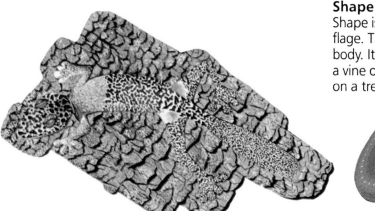

Pattern
The spade-tailed gecko has a mottled pattern that blends in well with the patchy bark of trees.

Unseen in the shadows
Rudyard Kipling's exciting story *The Jungle Book* (1894) tells of how a boy, the 'man-cub' Mowgli, is reared by a family of wolves in the jungles of India. One of the main characters is Kaa, a cunning and untrustworthy python. A troop of wild monkeys capture Mowgli. But Kaa arrives to help rescue him, and the monkeys are terrified. They know the stories of the great python who 'could slip along the branches as quietly as the moss grows – and who could make himself look so like a dead branch or a rotten stump that the wisest were deceived, till the branch caught them.' Such camouflage is even more effective at twilight and during the night, when many snakes go hunting.

Startle colors
The bright colors of many reptiles warn predators that they are venomous or that their flesh tastes horrible. This is called warning coloration. Bright colors are also used to startle an enemy. The blue-tongued skink (right) is a lizard. When threatened, it opens its mouth wide to reveal a bright blue tongue. The frilled lizard (top left) also flashes startle colors.

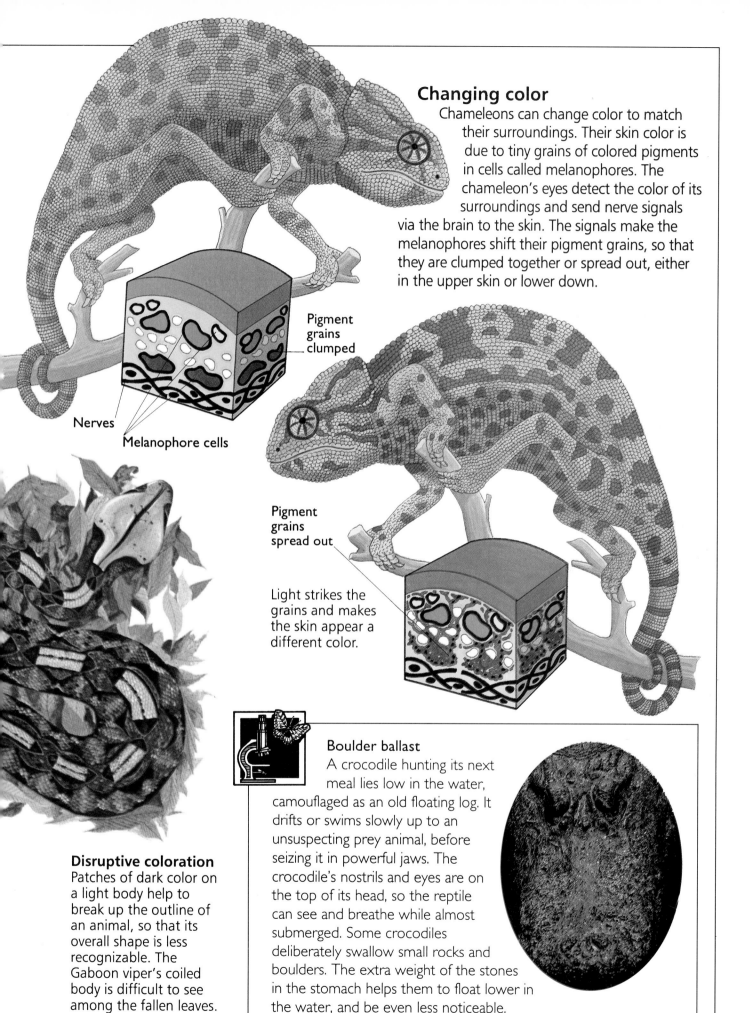

Changing color

Chameleons can change color to match their surroundings. Their skin color is due to tiny grains of colored pigments in cells called melanophores. The chameleon's eyes detect the color of its surroundings and send nerve signals via the brain to the skin. The signals make the melanophores shift their pigment grains, so that they are clumped together or spread out, either in the upper skin or lower down.

Pigment grains clumped

Nerves

Melanophore cells

Pigment grains spread out

Light strikes the grains and makes the skin appear a different color.

Disruptive coloration

Patches of dark color on a light body help to break up the outline of an animal, so that its overall shape is less recognizable. The Gaboon viper's coiled body is difficult to see among the fallen leaves.

Boulder ballast

A crocodile hunting its next meal lies low in the water, camouflaged as an old floating log. It drifts or swims slowly up to an unsuspecting prey animal, before seizing it in powerful jaws. The crocodile's nostrils and eyes are on the top of its head, so the reptile can see and breathe while almost submerged. Some crocodiles deliberately swallow small rocks and boulders. The extra weight of the stones in the stomach helps them to float lower in the water, and be even less noticeable.

DAILY LIFE

Reptiles are 'cold-blooded' animals; they cannot generate body heat inside their bodies, as mammals and birds do. If a reptile gets too cool, its body processes slow down, and it becomes sluggish and still. It cannot feed or escape from predators. So a reptile tries to maintain its body above a certain temperature through its behavior. Much of its daily life is spent moving from cool places to warm ones and back again, to keep the body within the best temperature range.

Coping with cold-bloodedness

Although reptiles are called 'cold-blooded,' a lizard or snake basking in tropical sunlight would have blood which is hotter than "warm-blooded" creatures such as mammals and birds. A better term is *ectothermic*. This means that warmth for the body comes from the outside – from the Sun. Through the day, the reptile positions and places itself to warm up or cool down, as necessary. If everywhere becomes too cold, for example, in the middle of the night, the reptile hides away for safety.

Midday
After a morning meal of insects and worms, the lizard gets too hot at noon. So it sits in the shade of a rock to cool down.

◀ **Dawn**
After the cool night, a lizard sits out in the early rays of the Sun. It soaks up the warmth and raises its body temperature.

Harnessing solar power
The Sun is a reliable and readily available source of energy. Many ectothermic animals rely on its warmth, from reptiles to insects and spiders. Plants rely on the Sun too, capturing its light energy by the process of photosynthesis. Humans have also recently discovered how to harness heat and light from the Sun, and convert it into electricity. We do this with devices ranging from light-powered calculators to huge solar furnaces and solar power plants, right.

Evening

In the evening the lizard stands side-on to the Sun to catch the last rays of warmth.

Night-time

As the Sun sets, the air and rocks become cool. The lizard returns to its burrow, as its movements slow.

◀ Afternoon

The lizard hunts during late afternoon. The amazing striking speed of snakes and lizards is only possible with warmed-up muscles.

Reptiles in the stars

Ancient peoples spent long hours observing the night sky. They imagined that patterns of stars traced the outlines of mythical characters, animals, and familiar objects. Recognizing these patterns, or star constellations, helped them to navigate across featureless oceans and unfamiliar landscapes. Several constellations are named after mythical reptiles: Draco the dragon, Hydra the sea serpent, Hydrus the water snake, Lacerta the lizard, Serpens the snake, and Ophiuchus the serpent-holder.

Winter sleep

The temperate zones of the world, such as Britain, and the middle regions of Europe and North America, have warm summers and cool winters. The winter temperatures are usually too low for reptiles to stay active. So they hide away in burrows and caves, or under logs and rocks. They enter a period of 'winter sleep' known as torpor, until the rising temperatures of spring rouse them.

Reptile worship

Several peoples have worshiped reptilian animals as gods or spirits. In ancient times in the Mexico region, people prayed to the feathered serpent god known as Quetzalcóatl.

FOOD AND FEEDING

Reptiles are mostly meat-eaters. They often snap up their small prey alive and swallow it whole, since they do not have effective chewing and crushing teeth, nor flexible cheeks and lips to hold the food in the mouth as they chew. Some lizards eat soft leaves and fruits, and some scavenge on dying and dead plants and animals. Komodo dragons (shown left) are large lizards that feed mainly on dead meat such as goat. Only a fraction of lizard species eat chiefly plants. Turtles and tortoises also consume plant material.

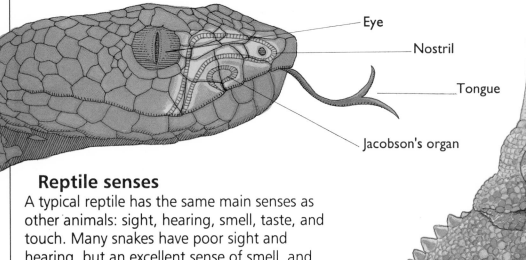

Eye

Nostril

Tongue

Jacobson's organ

Reptile senses

A typical reptile has the same main senses as other animals: sight, hearing, smell, taste, and touch. Many snakes have poor sight and hearing, but an excellent sense of smell, and can also detect vibrations through the ground. Some snakes use their tongues to smell, as well as touch and taste. The snake flicks out its tongue to gather particles of odors floating in the air. Then it puts its tongue to the roof of its mouth. Here a special part, Jacobson's organ, detects the scent.

Milking snakes

In some parts of the world, poisonous snakes (see page 22) have venom that is strong enough to kill humans. To develop an antivenom that counteracts the effects of the poison, and saves lives if given in time, snake experts need to study and test the poison itself. One way of obtaining it is to 'milk' the snake of its poison. The snake bites a container through its thin plastic top (shown right) and the poison dribbles from its fangs and collects in the bottom. The poison can then be analyzed in the laboratory.

Capturing food

The stealthy chameleon (left) creeps up to a victim such as a fly. Then it flicks out its long tongue. The victim sticks to the sticky tongue tip, and the chameleon whisks its tongue back into its mouth, swallowing the meal. This all happens too fast for us to see. The crocodile (below) must get close enough to grab a victim such as a zebra. Tortoises (below right) are too slow to chase victims. They munch leaves most of the day.

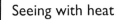

Seeing with heat

Under their eyes, pit vipers have pit organs that can detect heat. The snake uses these organs to search for warm-blooded prey such as mice and birds. The snake can form an image of the prey and strike at it, even in darkness.

Reptile cuisine

Reptile meat is a popular food in some parts of the world. Some Chinese dishes contain quick-cooked snake meat. Australian aboriginals hunt and eat large goannas, types of monitor lizards.

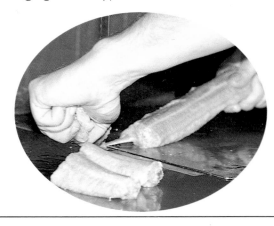

Gone fishin'

Human anglers may pride themselves on their fishing skills. But some kinds of reptiles have been fishing with bait for millions of years. The alligator snapping turtle of North America lies still on the lake bed with its mouth open to reveal a red 'worm,' part of its tongue, which wriggles invitingly. Small fish investigate the worm, and are snapped up by powerful jaws.

COURTSHIP AND BREEDING

Reptiles breed in much the same way as other vertebrates (animals with backbones). A male and female of the same species locate one another, court, and mate. The female then lays a clutch of eggs, usually in a safe place. The babies develop inside the eggs, living on stores of food, and hatch out after several weeks. In some types of snakes, the babies are born fully formed. In some species, the parents look after the young, but parental care in reptiles is much less common than in birds and mammals.

Competition

Male Nile monitor lizards wrestle with each other. The most powerful win the contest and mate with the females. This helps to ensure the fittest, strongest males father the next generation.

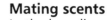

Mating scents

In the breeding season, a female snake gives off a mating scent. This attracts several males who crawl over her. They twine and wrap around each other, until the strongest and most persistent wins and mates with her.

The dragon dance

In China dragons are ancient symbols of fertility. People make model dragons and dance inside them in street processions and carnivals. The aim was traditionally to encourage families to grow and stay healthy, farm animals to breed, crops to grow, and trees to bear fruit.

The caring crocodile

For many years, crocodiles were thought to be cannibals that fed on the young of their own kind. This was because they were seen with babies in their mouths. Then careful observation showed that the crocodiles were, in fact, mothers. They were looking after their newly hatched babies, guarding them and carrying them to the water. Few predators would dare try to snatch a baby from those ferocious teeth! This is a rare case of parental care in reptiles.

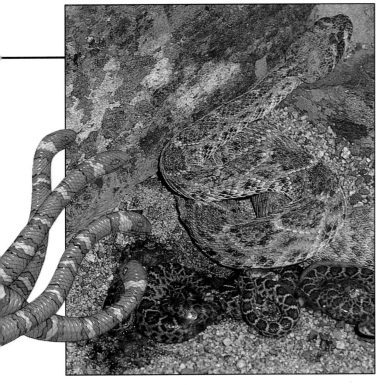

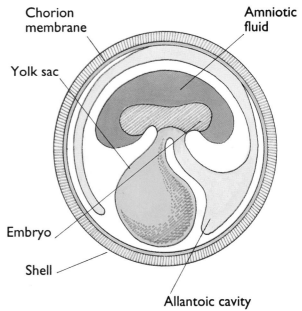

Chorion membrane

Amniotic fluid

Yolk sac

Embryo

Shell

Allantoic cavity

Inside the egg

Inside each egg, the embryo (developing baby) has its own private 'pond' of amniotic fluid. Most of the food store is in the form of yolk, while the baby's body wastes collect in the chamber called the allantoic cavity. The baby can 'breathe' through the shell – the oxygen necessary for life seeps through tiny holes or pores in the shell, and into blood passing through the chorion layer. In some types of snakes, the eggshell never develops fully and the babies grow inside their mother's body. They are born as fully formed, tiny versions of their parents (above left). In many turtles, the eggs are laid in the warm sand of a riverbank or beach (left). The warmth speeds their development.

Saving the turtles
Vacationers flock to the sandy beaches of islands in the Caribbean, Mediterranean, and Southeast Asia. These beaches are also visited by sea turtles to lay their eggs. Wildlife campaigners want them to be declared nature reserves, but local people do not want to lose the vacation trade.

CROCODILES AND ALLIGATORS

The 22 species of crocodilians are all lurking predators, which also scavenge meat from any dead carcass left by another hunter. They live in tropical regions, in or near water, and spend much of the day basking in the sun to keep warm. The powerful tail and rear limbs are used to propel the animal through the water. The caimans of South America have the shortest, broadest snouts and eat the most varied diet, including frogs, snakes, lizards, birds, and mammals. The gavial of the Indian region has a long, narrow snout and eats mainly fish.

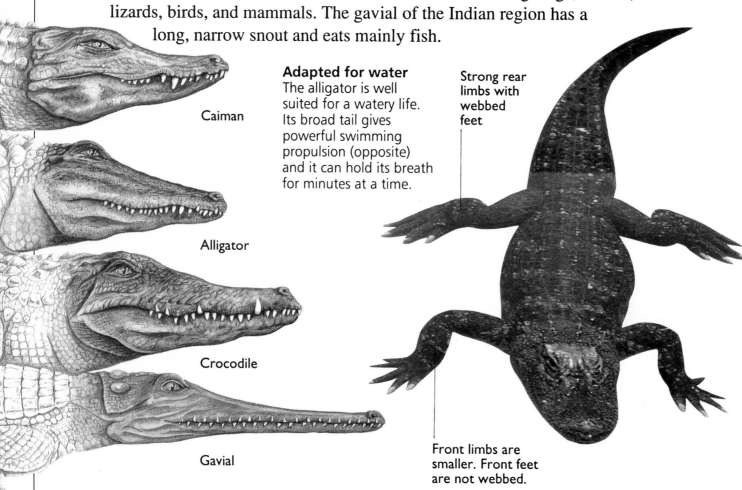

Caiman

Alligator

Crocodile

Gavial

Adapted for water
The alligator is well suited for a watery life. Its broad tail gives powerful swimming propulsion (opposite) and it can hold its breath for minutes at a time.

Strong rear limbs with webbed feet

Front limbs are smaller. Front feet are not webbed.

Crocodilians worldwide
The map shows the distribution of some of the main species of crocodilians. The two main groups are the crocodiles, with 14 species, and alligators, with 7 species, which includes the caimans. The Estuarine crocodile is the only one that lives in salt water.

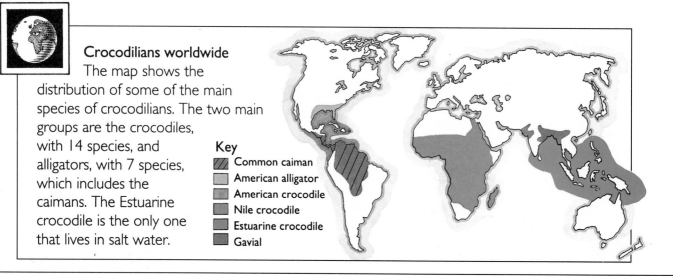

Key
- Common caiman
- American alligator
- American crocodile
- Nile crocodile
- Estuarine crocodile
- Gavial

The swishing tail

The tail is arched from side to side by powerful muscles running down the animal's body. The main part of the body is relatively stiff and takes little part in swimming.

With a crocodile's help

The crocodile features in many stories. In *The Just So Stories* by Rudyard Kipling (1902) a crocodile seizes a young elephant by its nose, which is 'no bigger than a boot.' The elephant tries to get away, and its nose stretches – which is how, supposedly, the elephant got its trunk!

From rare to common

American alligators live in the southeastern United States. They were hunted so much for their skins and because they threatened people and livestock, that they became in danger of extinction (dying out completely). Wildlife laws were introduced in 1969 to protect them. In 1987 the species was declared to be out of danger of extinction. Today they are more common and a few are hunted (below).

Crocodile swimming

The main swimming power for crocodilians comes from the deep tail, which swishes from side to side like a fish's tail. This pushes the animal forward. The front legs are usually held up against the underside of the body, for better streamlining. The rear legs can be used for steering, and for paddling at slow speeds. By thrusting its rear feet forward and up, with its webbed toes spread, a crocodile can suddenly stop moving forward and sink down under the water.

Crocodile songs

Crocodilians feature in various plays and also in popular songs. These include *See You Later Alligator* (1956), the early rock'n'roll jive-talking hit by Bill Haley and the Comets, and *Crocodile Rock* (1973) by Elton John.

Bill Haley

POISONOUS SNAKES

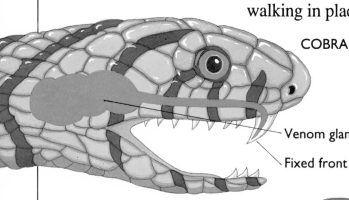

There are nearly 2,400 species of snakes around the world. But only about one-sixth of these have venom (poison) strong enough to harm other creatures. Only a few dozen have venom powerful enough to seriously harm or kill a person. Poisonous snakes use their venom to paralyze or kill their prey. Occasionally they will bite in self-defense, for example, if a careless person treads on them. Just in case, it is best to treat all snakes with respect, and to take great care when walking in places where snakes live.

COBRA

Venom gland

Fixed front fangs

Front fangs hinge forward to strike

VIPER

Venom

Venom and fangs

Snake venom is made in venom glands on either side of the head. The snake injects its venom into the victim when it bites, using its long teeth, called fangs. Back-fanged snakes such as the deadly boomslang and the twig snake have grooved fangs at the rear of the mouth. Cobras, including coral snakes, have fangs at the front. Vipers, including adders, sidewinders and rattlesnakes, have long, hinged fangs that fold back when not in use.

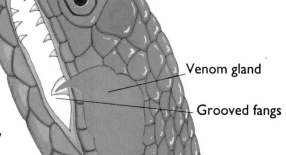

BOOMSLANG

Venom gland

Grooved fangs

Snake charming

In some parts of the world people 'charm' snakes by playing flute music, as the snake sways to and fro, as though dancing or hypnotized. Often poisonous snakes such as cobras are used, though they sometimes have their venom glands or fangs removed. In fact, the snake can hardly hear the flute. It may react to the rocking body of the charmer and to the vibrations from his or her tapping foot.

Above: Coral snake

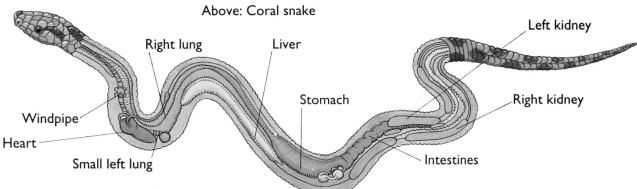

Right lung

Liver

Left kidney

Windpipe

Heart

Stomach

Right kidney

Small left lung

Intestines

Mimicry
Some poisonous snakes advertise their identity with bright warning colors so that other animals do not attack. Certain nonpoisonous snakes have similar colors. They are mimics, pretending to be dangerous, so that they fool enemies and gain the same protection.

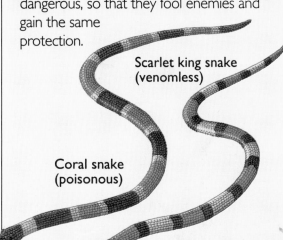

Scarlet king snake (venomless)

Coral snake (poisonous)

Inside a snake
Snakes are long and thin. Their internal organs have an unusual design, to fit within the body shape. Instead of two lungs side by side, there is only one working lung, the right one. The left lung is either very small or absent altogether. The right kidney is in front of the left one.

NONPOISONOUS SNAKES

The vast majority of the world's snakes are not poisonous. They live quiet, secretive lives in wild and remote places such as jungles, swamps, and deserts. They hunt small creatures such as insects, spiders, worms, mice, and frogs, and rarely come in contact with people. The smallest are as short as your finger. There are a few giant species, such as pythons and anacondas, but their size and power have been often exaggerated. Like most reptiles, snakes never stop growing, although their growth rate slows when they are old.

Egg-eating snake

A big meal
No snake can bite or chew pieces from its prey. It swallows the victim whole. So it has a jaw joint with a double hinge, and elastic ligaments connecting the jaw bones. These allow the snake's mouth to stretch so much that it can swallow a meal bigger than its head.

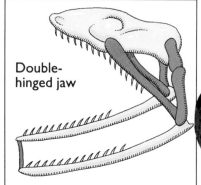

Double-hinged jaw

Pythons and boas
Two groups of snakes squeeze their prey to death. These groups are the pythons, with 27 species, and the boas, with 39 species. These were probably among the first snakes to evolve, more than 70 million years ago. They still have tiny remnants of rear limb bones embedded in the body.

Sign of healing
In ancient Greece, Asclepius was the god of medicine. His father, the sun god Apollo, taught him the art of healing. According to legend the sacred snakes of Asclepius licked the wounds of sick people, so the symbol of two serpents twined around a staff became the sign of medicine.

Death by suffocation
A python or boa wraps its body around the prey and tightens. When the prey breathes out and its chest shrinks, the snake tightens its grip. The prey's chest is squashed and it dies from suffocation.

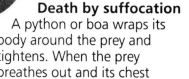

Dead and alive

Several species of snake 'play dead' when threatened. The grass snake (above) flops onto the ground, often on its back, and goes loose and limp, with its tongue lolling out. The attacker is often so surprised that it moves away.

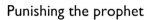

Punishing the prophet

The Laocoön is a famous sculpture from the time of ancient Greece. It is about 2,000 years old. It shows Laocoön, a Trojan priest who foretold the destruction of Troy. In punishment, Laocoön and his sons were attacked by sea snakes. Forgotten for centuries, the statue was dug up in 1506.

Rectilinear motion

The wide, flat scales on the python's belly are close together and overlapping. The rear of the body grips the ground.

The python stretches the front part of its body.

It lowers the scales to grip the ground.

Green tree boa

Biggest and smallest

From reliable records, the world's longest snake is a reticulated python, from Southeast Asia, at 32 ft 9 in (10 m). The heaviest snake is the anaconda from South America. It weighs over 600 lb (270 kg) when 30 ft (9 m) long. The longest poisonous snake is the king cobra, at 18 ft 9 in (5.72 m). The smallest snake is a type of thread snake from the West Indies, at about 4 in (10 cm).

Young thread snake

Eat dust, snake!

Many cultures have regarded snakes as evil and cunning, perhaps because their body shape and movement is so different to ours. In the Bible's Old Testament, God creates Adam and Eve, the first man and woman, in the Garden of Eden. A mysterious serpent tempts Eve to eat the forbidden fruit of the garden, and so brings sin to the world. Eve says to God: 'The serpent beguiled me, and I did eat..' So God tells the serpent that it is cursed: 'Upon thy belly thou shalt go, and dust thou shalt eat all the days of thy life.'

LIZARDS

The lizard group is by far the biggest group of reptiles living today, and the most widespread around the world. In many regions, especially the tropics, lizards are a familiar sight. They hunt mainly by day, in the open, so people see them more often than other reptiles. Lizards do not have poisonous bites, except for two North American species, the gila monster and the Mexican beaded lizard. Some species, such as the Australian frilled lizard, have evolved elaborate crests or frills, to make themselves look fiercer to enemies, or to impress their mates.

Shape and form

Most lizards have a large head with prominent eyes, a slim body, four legs of equal length, and a long tail. However, this basic body shape has become adapted in many different ways, to suit various lifestyles. Some lizards that burrow rapidly in soft soil have lost their limbs, and look more like snakes. Some lizards have strong, agile limbs and grasping fingers, for moving through the branches.

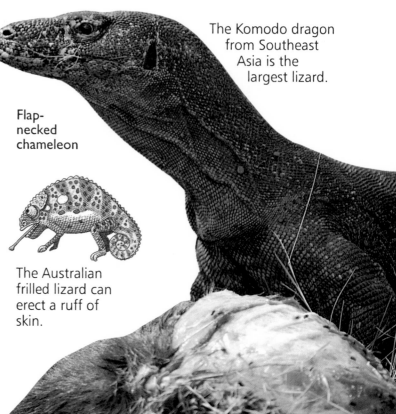

The Komodo dragon from Southeast Asia is the largest lizard.

Flap-necked chameleon

The Australian frilled lizard can erect a ruff of skin.

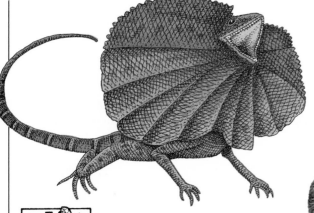

Impressing a mate

The anole lizard from South and Central America is one of many species in which the male is larger and more brightly colored than the female. He can display a flap of skin on his throat, known as the dewlap, by moving his throat bone forward to hold the flap out like a fan. The dewlap is vivid red or yellow, and its flash of color tells the female that he is courting her and wishes to mate. Flying lizards have a similar dewlap.

Disposable tail

A lizard's tail is useful as a counterbalance, when climbing over rocks or branches. But it is not vital for survival. If a predator grabs the tail, the lizard tightens its tail muscles at a special point, so that the tail snaps off. The lizard escapes, the muscles spasm to prevent too much bleeding, and a new tail gradually grows.

Spiny-tailed lizard from Africa and Southern Asia

Animal distribution

Like many other land animals, lizards show distinct patterns of distribution. In other words, the group of animal species found in one area is different from that found in another. In the 1850's the English naturalist Alfred Russel Wallace studied animal distribution. Wallace proposed an imaginary line separating the animal life of Australasia from that of Southeast Asia, as shown below.

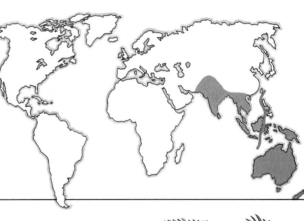

S E Asian species
Australasian species

Tegu lizard from South America

Galapagos marine iguana

Female-only lizards

In some kinds of animals there are no males at all, only females. This is fairly common among insects and worms, and also occurs in lizards. The females are able to lay eggs which hatch into young without first mating with a male. This method of reproduction is called parthenogenesis. The New Mexico whiptail lizard is parthenogenetic. It has been bred in captivity for many generations, with no males at all.

TURTLES AND TORTOISES

The chelonians – turtles, tortoises, and terrapins – are probably the most distinctive group of reptiles. With their hard, heavy shells, they are living proof that the slow-but-armored way of life can be very successful. Fossils show that the first chelonians appeared on Earth over 200 million years ago, almost before mammals and dinosaurs evolved. Today they live in many places, from deserts to rainforests and the sea, and across the tropical and temperate zones of the world.

A clue to evolution

English naturalist Charles Darwin began to think about how animals evolve when he visited the Galapagos Islands in the Pacific, in the 1830's. He noticed that each island had its own type of giant tortoise. In 1859 Darwin's book *On the Origin of Species* caused great controversy. This theory has since become a central part of biology.

Heroes in a half-shell

In the 1980s animated cartoons featuring the Teenage Mutant Ninja Turtles became popular. The Ninja Turtles were supposed to have mutated (changed) due to radioactive wastes, from small pet turtles into pizza-eating, crime-busting heroes.

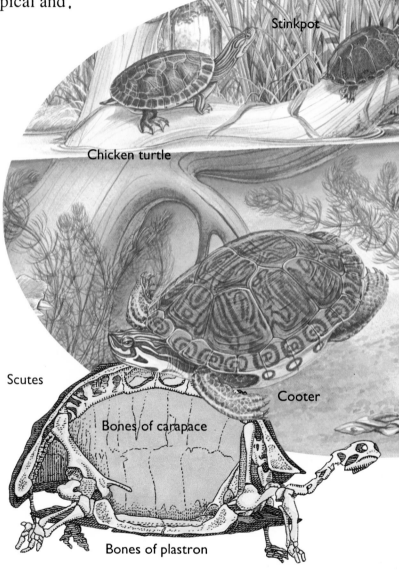

Stinkpot

Chicken turtle

Scutes

Cooter

Bones of carapace

Bones of plastron

Inside a turtle

The chelonian shell is made from about 60 bony plates fused together. Those on the back form a dome called the carapace. Those underneath form a flatter bowl, the plastron. The ribs and backbones are stuck to the inside of the carapace. Large, scale-like scutes strengthen the outside of the shell.

Tortoiseshell crafts
Many small items today, such as combs, small boxes, and patterned jewellery, are made from plastics. In the past, people around the world used the strong, smoothed, polished shells of tortoises and turtles, known by the general name of tortoiseshell, to make similar items. However, this trade has made several chelonians very rare, and it is now controlled.

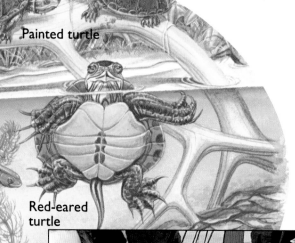

Painted turtle

Red-eared turtle

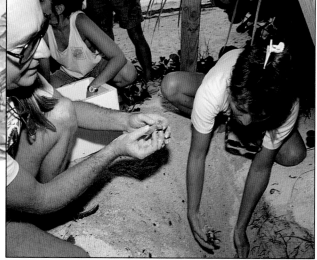

The warm swamps of Florida are ideal for chelonians (left). Some are plant-eaters, but many are hunters, digging for shellfish and worms in the mud, or snapping at fish and snakes. The gopher tortoise (above) has a different lifestyle, burrowing underground.

Soup's up!
In the days of sailing ships, sailors caught slow-swimming sea turtles and kept them in the ship's hold. The turtles, being hardy creatures, stayed alive for weeks, and provided fresh meat when they were killed. Turtle soup was a popular, tasty, and nutritious dish.

Conservation
Chelonians are some of the most endangered of reptiles, and indeed, of all animals. They have been hunted for their meat, and for the tortoiseshell material from their shells. Their breeding places are disturbed by tourism (see page 19). Dozens of chelonians and other threatened reptiles are now on the lists of endangered species protected by law and by conservationists (above).

REPTILE CLASSIFICATION

The reptiles form the class (major animal group) called Reptilia. Their closest relatives are the classes of amphibians, birds, and mammals. The total number of reptile species is just over 6,500. This figure may rise slowly as new species, especially small lizards, are discovered in remote and inaccessible places. However, at the same time, destruction of places such as tropical rainforests is almost certainly making some species extinct. This could be happening even before reptile experts can discover, study, and name them.

Crocs, alligators, caimans, gavial 22 species, 0.3% of total

Nile croc

Tuatara 2 species, 0.03% of total

Worm-lizards 140 species, 2% of total

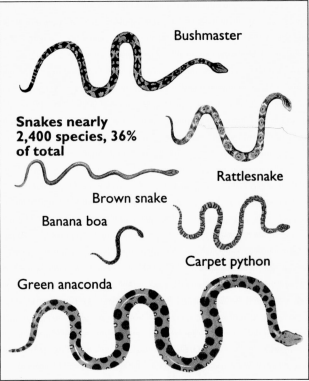

Bushmaster

Snakes nearly 2,400 species, 36% of total

Rattlesnake

Brown snake

Banana boa

Carpet python

Green anaconda

Turtles, tortoises, terrapins approx 244 species, 4% of total

Green turtle

Leopard tortoise

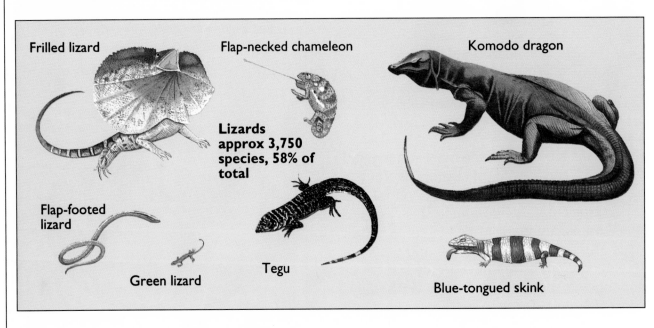

Frilled lizard

Flap-necked chameleon

Komodo dragon

Lizards approx 3,750 species, 58% of total

Flap-footed lizard

Green lizard

Tegu

Blue-tongued skink

GLOSSARY

Adaptation Special features that enable an animal such as a reptile to survive in a particular place.

Camouflage Patterns, colors, and shapes on an animal's body which make it blend in with its surroundings, so that it is difficult to see.

Carnivore An animal that eats mainly meat.

Classification The method used by scientists to group together animals that share similar characteristics.

Cells The microscopic building blocks which make up all living things.

Cold-blooded See Ectothermic.

Disruptive coloration Colors and patterns on an animal's body which break up its body outline, making it less visible to potential prey or predators.

Ectothermic An animal which cannot generate its own body heat, and which therefore cannot remain active if the temperature of its surroundings is too cold or hot.

Evolution The process by which animals (and plants) adapt to form new species that are better suited to their environment. Evolution usually takes place gradually, over thousands of millions of years, as individuals that are best suited to their habitat survive and reproduce, whilst those that are less well suited die out.

Habitat The kind of place where an animal lives and to which its body is adapted, such as desert, forest, scrubland, or seashore.

Herbivore An animal that eats mostly plant material, such as leaves, stems, roots, or fruit.

Hibernation Winter sleep, or torpor

Locomotion Method of movement from one place to another, such as running, swimming, or jumping.

Mammal An animal that has hair (fur) and feeds its young on milk.

Mimicry The action of pretending to be another animal, often because it is harmful and the mimic is harmless.

Parthenogenesis In female animals, the ability to reproduce without first being fertilized by a male.

Predator An animal which hunts and eats other animals for food.

Prey Animal hunted for food by a predator.

Sluffing The process by which snakes and some species of lizards molt or shed the outer layer of skin at once, rather than gradually, as most animals do.

Species A group of living things with the same characteristics, that breed together.

Startle colors Bright colors on an animal's body that are usually hidden, but which can be revealed to surprise an enemy and ward off attack.

Vertebrate An animal with an internal skeleton and a backbone, or spine.

Warm-blooded An animal whose internal body temperature remains constant whatever the temperature of its surroundings, so that it can remain active in hot or cold weather.

Warning coloration Distinctive patterns and colors that warn potential predators that an animal is poisonous or tastes horrible.

INDEX

Photocredits

Abbreviations: t-top, m-middle, b-bottom, l-left, r-right
Cover t, 3b, 12, 18, 21br: Spectrum; cover b: Roger Vlitos; 2, 5 both, 6-7, 15, 21t, 28t: Mary Evans Picture Library; 3m, 4, 9b, 17 all, 26m: Planet Earth Pictures; 6t, 7r, 11m and b, 16 both, 19 all, 24, 25b, 26t and b, 27, 29m: Bruce Coleman; 6b, 7l, 29br: Hulton Deutsch; 9t, 14t, 22: NHPA; 10, 11t, 13, 20b, 28b, 29t and bl: Frank Spooner Pictures; 14b: Scandia; 20t: Frank Lane; 25t: Bridgeman Art Library.